Drive and Stroll i

Somerset

Drive and Stroll in

Somerset

•

Roger Evans

COUNTRYSIDE BOOKS
NEWBURY BERKSHIRE

COUNTRYSIDE BOOKS
3 Catherine Road
Newbury, Berkshire

To view our complete range of books
please visit us at
www.countrysidebooks.co.uk

ISBN 1 85306 961 2
EAN 978 1 85306 961 1

Cover picture of Allerford supplied by David Sellman
Designed by Peter Davies, Nautilus Design

Typeset by Mac Style, Nafferton, E. Yorkshire
Produced through MRM Associates Ltd., Reading
Printed by Borcombe Printers, Romsey

Contents

Area Map Showing the Locations of the Walks

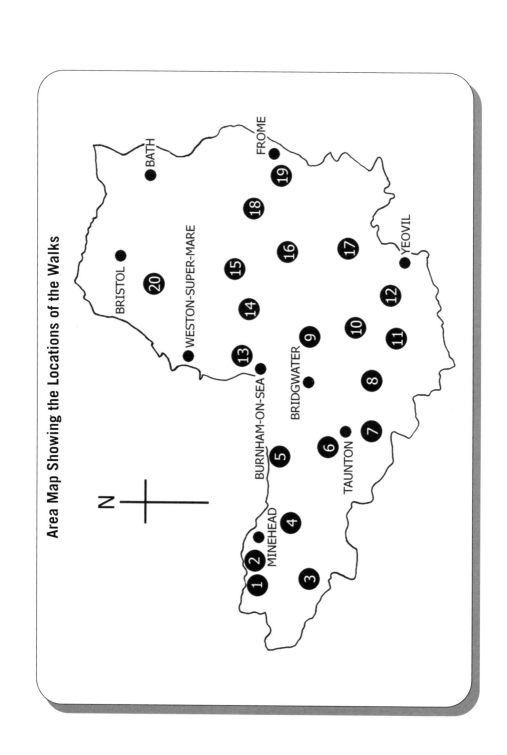

Contents

PUBLISHER'S NOTE

We hope that you obtain considerable enjoyment from this book; great care has been taken in its preparation. Although at the time of publication all routes followed public rights of way or permitted paths, diversion orders can be made and permissions withdrawn

We cannot, of course, be held responsible for such diversion orders and any inaccuracies in the text which result from these or any other changes to the routes nor any damage which might result from walkers trespassing on private property. We are anxious, though, that all details covering the walks are kept up to date and would therefore welcome information from readers which would be relevant to future editions.

The simple sketch maps that accompany the walks in this book are based on notes made by the author whilst checking out the routes on the ground. They are designed to show you how to reach the start, to point out the main features of the overall circuit and they contain a progression of numbers that relate to the paragraphs of the text.

However, for the benefit of a proper map, we do recommend that you purchase the relevant Ordnance Survey sheet covering your walk. The Ordnance survey maps are widely available, especially through booksellers and local newsagents.

Introduction

Allerford

I recently drove my ninety-two-year-old mother through our home town and she commented on how it had altered over the years, barely recognisable as the place in which she came to live in 1942. 'Everything's changing,' she said. Town centres are transformed and the urban boundaries creep unrelentingly into the countryside, housing estates consuming the green belt without mercy. But drive out into the countryside of Somerset, into the heart of Exmoor, the Quantocks or Mendips, and you enter an unchanging world with country inns still serving the needs of the traveller as they did decades ago. The footpaths and bridleways I walk today are those that my grandparents once trod. The inns are those in which our grandparents once took their refreshments. This is the unspoilt Somerset with its feeling of constancy that you will find in these countryside walks.

In this book I hope to reveal some of the tracks and byways I have enjoyed around the county where a suitable inn complements a country stroll. The walks, all circular and between 2 miles and 5$^1/_2$ miles in length, cover the full range of Somerset's scenery, the high and hilly moorland, the low and flat levels, the wooded combes and the glorious coastline. Whilst the routes vary in length, the longest are also the flattest, the intention being that the reader should be able to relax and enjoy a stroll. So I invite you to join me on some of my favourite walks in Somerset's varied and wonderful landscape.

Roger Evans

1 | Culbone and Robber's Bridge

The Culbone Inn is passed on the walk

The Walk: 4 miles 🕐 2 hours
Map: OS Explorer OL9 Exmoor (GR 841462)

How to get there

Pittcombe Head, the start point for this walk, is on the A39 between Porlock and Lynton – look for an AA phone box at the brow of a hill on the main road. It is on the left travelling west from Porlock or on the right if travelling from Lynton. **Parking:** The car park is the off-road area immediately across the road from the AA box. This also provides a picnic area. Alternative parking can be found at Robber's Bridge (point 2) and the Culbone Inn offers parking for patrons.

Drive and Stroll

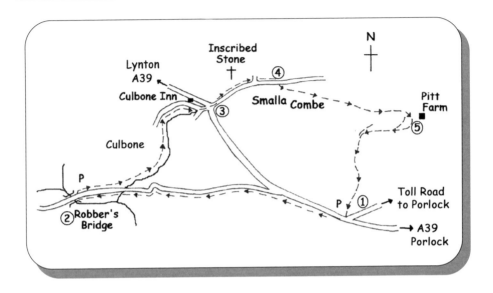

Introduction

This delightful walk takes a glimpse at that part of Exmoor which lies to the west of Lynmouth and Porlock. It includes the village of Culbone and the picturesque Robber's Bridge. Culbone can boast the smallest parish church in England, just 35 feet long, possibly the earliest church on Exmoor. With no road access, it can only be reached on foot.

Robber's Bridge crosses Weir Water, one of numerous streams that cascade down the deep-sided, heavily wooded valleys. Further downstream is the hamlet of Oare, with its church where Lorna Doone of Blackmore's novel was shot through the window. It is from the villainous Doone family that Robber's Bridge is believed to take its name. Whilst Lorna may have been a fictitious character, the Doones were not. Villains aside, the bridge is set in some of the most beautiful scenery in the West Country and it is the walker who really benefits from its lack of vehicular access. The final leg of the walk, to the east of Culbone, passes through heavily forested valleys and provides welcome shade on the uphill stretch to the car park.

The Culbone Inn

This was once the Culbone Stables, a staging post at which horses were changed on the Minehead to Barnstaple stagecoach route, believed to have been the last one running in the country. Eventually it became a club but was converted to an inn after the Second World War.

Reached at point 3 of the walk, real ales and a choice of bar meals are available, with seating both inside and out. There are wonderful views down the combe leading to Robber's Bridge. The inn is so high up that there is no mains water supply, hence all the water used at the inn is natural spring water.

For those who have an interest in the Beast of Exmoor, it is worth looking beneath the trees in the grounds of the inn! Don't be surprised by what you see. Telephone: 01643 862259.

THE WALK

Leave the car park by turning right onto the main road. In 500 yards, turn left taking the minor road, which leads downhill for about a mile to reach **Robber's Bridge**.

Before the bridge, turn right onto a footpath signposted 'Culbone Stables and A39'. Walk uphill along the side of the valley to a gate. Follow the path as it curves left, keeping the stream at the bottom of **Met Combe** to your right. The path then bears right and passes through an avenue of trees before going through a gate and leading up to the A39, to the right of the clearly visible **Culbone Inn**.

Cross the main road and take the lane opposite, signposted to **Yarner and Ash Farms**, passing over a cattle grid.

Notice the fenced area to your left, which contains the Culbone Stone. Discovered in 1940, it is a 3 foot high feature supporting a wheeled cross and possibly dates back to the 7th century. It is listed as an ancient monument and is not far off the route for those interested in taking this diversion. To visit the stone, cross the stile, turn right to follow the fence line and then turn left where indicated by a signpost.

Back on the road, go past a 'Private, no entry' lane to your left. Shortly after this, the road bears right.

A rare sight on the A39

Just before the road bears left, take the bridleway path to the right signposted 'Porlock Weir 2'. This takes you into the steep-sided, wooded **Smalla Combe**. Follow the path down the combe, with the stream to your right, until the path naturally crosses the stream. Continue to follow the stream downhill, with it now to your left until just before **Pitt Farm**.

At the farm, follow the yellow waymarked sign to **Pittcombe Head**. Almost immediately take the right-hand uphill path at the fork, again bearing right at the next fork. Continue uphill along the obvious path, ignoring any tracks merging from either side.

Dog walkers please note: Along this section the forestry area is fenced on your left-hand side. About 6 inches off the ground is an electric fence to control rabbits. It also controls low-lying dogs, which may sniff it! Nature lovers may also note the occasional opening to allow other creatures through such as hedgehogs, weasels etc.

Approaching the brow of the hill, pass though the pedestrian gate alongside a metal gate to reach the car park.

2 | Porlock Weir and Porlock

Porlock Weir

The Walk: 4 miles ⏱ 2 hours
Map: OS Explorer OL9 Exmoor (GR 865478)

How to get there

Porlock is on the A39 between Minehead and Lynmouth. From the centre of Porlock take the road signposted to West Porlock and Porlock Weir, the B3225. Continue to the very end of the road where you will find the Ship Inn. **Parking:** The pay and display car park is at the very end of the Porlock Weir road, just opposite the Ship Inn.

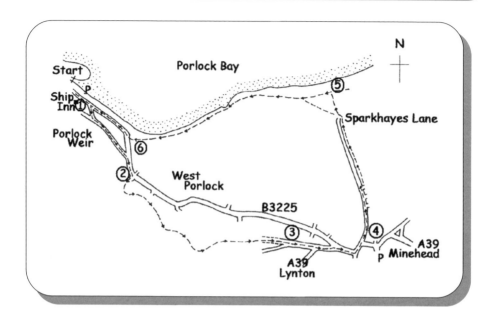

Introduction

The walk provides a pleasant mix of woodland and coastal walking. At one time the sea went in all the way to Porlock, now over $1/2$ mile inland. As the water retreated, so Porlock Weir was created out of necessity around 1422. The cottage called Oyster Perch is a reminder of the oyster beds here, a well kept local secret. It is worth walking around the cluster of cottages to discover buildings with considerable charm, including one built from an old limekiln.

Porlock lies along the narrowest section of the main A39. It offers a number of shops and tearooms at point 4, conveniently halfway along the route.

The Ship Inn, Porlock Weir

This is under the same ownership as the Anchor Hotel and each offers an unrivalled situation with views across Porlock Bay and the Weir. The 16th century Ship Inn is better suited to walkers and offers ample seating both inside and out. The outside tables are on the roadway but since the road is a dead end, it isn't a problem. This is a good country inn offering real ales and a choice of bar meals. Telephone: 01643 862753.

Drive and Stroll

THE WALK

Leave the car park and cross the road towards the **Ship Inn**. To the left of the inn, the road forks. Take the right-hand road, which leads uphill and, after bearing left, runs parallel with the road along which you drove into the village. This offers a traffic free route until you rejoin the main road. Turn right at the main road and continue for about 40 yards.

Where the road bears left, take the footpath which goes straight ahead, alongside a metal bench, signposted 'Bossington via Porlock'. In a short distance, go straight across a road, keeping to the left of the long wood-built hut, to follow the path uphill, signposted 'Bridleway to Porlock Hill, Footpath to Porlock'. Cross a stream using a footbridge (or wade across the ford) to follow the path, which bears left and climbs gently uphill. At a fork, the path then drops to the left, signposted to **Porlock**.

Ignore the path that goes straight ahead signposted as 'Horses to Porlock'.

At a crossroad of paths (**West Porlock** to the left, **Porlock Hill** to the right), go straight ahead towards **Porlock**, through a chicane stile.

Note the magnificent gardens on your left-hand side along the next stretch. They are wonderful throughout the spring and summer.

At the next junction, keep straight ahead, signposted to Porlock with a blue marker. Follow the fence line on your left, ignoring a track to the left at the end of a walled garden. The path eventually emerges onto a metalled road in **Porlock**.

Notice the fine views across Porlock Bay along this last stretch. It is easy to see how the sea has receded here, leaving the one-time coastal village of Porlock high and dry.

At the road, turn left and walk down to the A39 where you turn left again. Follow this through the **High Street**.

Turn left into **Sparkhayes Lane**. Follow this road until the end of the paved section. Take the slope to the right, which leads to a pedestrian gate alongside a farm gate. Pass through the gate and follow the footpath just inside the field boundary alongside the (unsafe) lane.

The 16th-century Ship Inn

Continue to the shoreline and, once there, turn left to follow the coastal path to **Porlock Weir**.

At low tide, evidence of a petrified sunken forest can be seen along the shore. The roots of the forest trees are believed to date back to 4000 BC.

Eventually you will rejoin the road after crossing a stile. Turn right to head back to the car park.

3 | Tarr Steps

The river crossing at Tarr Steps

The Walk: $2^1/_2$ miles ⏱ $1^1/_2$ hours
Map: OS Explorer OL9 Exmoor (GR 872324)

How to get there

Take the B3223, which runs between Simonsbath and Dulverton. About 5 miles north of Dulverton, turn off to head west, following the tourist signposts for Tarr Steps. Pass through the hamlet of Liscombe and continue following the signs for Tarr Steps. **Parking:** As you descend the hill towards Tarr Steps, there is a large car park on your left-hand side. This is the only parking option.

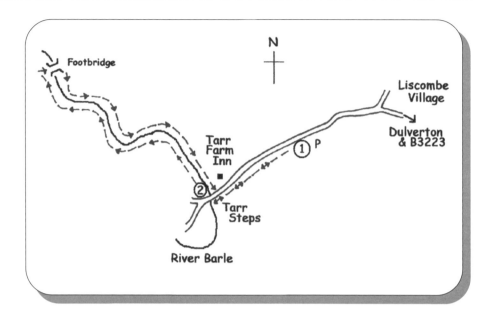

Introduction

This short and easy walk takes you across the ancient Tarr Steps to complete a riverside walk along the fast flowing Barle and through some beautiful and peaceful scenery. Tarr Steps is an ancient monument and the finest clapper bridge in England spanning 55 feet of river in 17 spans of flat stones.

The Tarr Farm Inn

The exterior of this 16th century inn clearly shows that it was once a farm but it now serves as a pub and tearooms. It is set high on a bank overlooking Tarr Steps, with ample seating to be found both inside and out. The bar offers a selection of real ales and a good range of food. In recent years additional buildings have been created providing overnight accommodation. Telephone: 01643 851507.

THE WALK

Leave the car park at the bottom end and follow the footpath down to where the **Tarr Steps clapper bridge** crosses the river. Go over the clapper bridge.

The largest of these stones is 8½ feet long and 5 feet wide. Their source is unknown but they are considered by some to date back to the Ice Age, an opinion perhaps inspired by the nearby presence of burial mounds of Bronze Age men from 5,000 years ago. Opinions on the age of the bridge differ but it is almost certainly medieval and for use by packhorse traders. These ancient stones form one of the oldest clapper bridges in England, which at one time was known as the Devil's Bridge.

Once across the river, turn right to follow the bank, walking upstream along a grass and stone track, with the water on your right. Continue until you come to a footbridge, which crosses the river.

Cross the bridge and turn right to follow the river downstream, keeping the water on your right. This leads you back to the clapper bridge where you turn left for the **Tarr Farm Inn** and the car park.

Tarr Farm Inn

4 Luxborough

The charming village of Luxborough

The Walk: 3 miles 🕐 1¹/₂ hours
Map: OS Explorer OL9 Exmoor (GR 985379)

How to get there

From the B3224, which runs across Exmoor between Raleigh's Cross and Wheddon Cross, take the signposted road north to Luxborough. Follow the road all the way into the village of Luxborough. At the Royal Oak, continue straight on, signposted to Roadwater, but first look left to see if there is any safe kerbside parking space across the road from the inn. This may be your alternative parking. Continue past the Royal Oak to where the road forks at Purley Ford. **Parking:** Just before the road fork at Purley Ford, there is a layby where you may park. If no space is available, then try opposite the inn. Parking is available at the inn for patrons.

Drive and Stroll

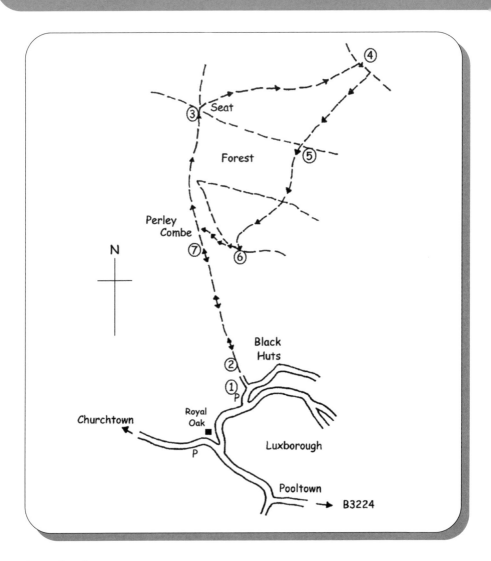

Introduction

This walk offers a nice climb up through Perley Combe and takes advantage of forestry roads. At the turn around point, there are fine views along the Somerset coast and across to the Welsh mountains. Luxborough is a small village where old fashioned cottages sit alongside a fast flowing stream. Its village hall, which can be seen from the inn, has a playing field adjoining it with picnic tables in a quiet, unspoilt setting.

The Royal Oak

This traditional rural inn is absolutely full of character. A wide selection of home-cooked, fresh food, which varies daily, and real ales are on offer. These can be taken in any one of a number of different rooms, the intimate Green Room and the sporting Red Room among them. Snacks are also served in one of the bars or can be enjoyed in the secluded garden. En-suite accommodation is available. Telephone: 01984 640319.

THE WALK

①

At the road fork, go to the left and pass a row of cottages. Shortly after, turn left onto a metalled road marked as 'Monkham Wood Depot'.

 ②

At some large black huts, the road becomes a stony track, which you follow uphill, along the edge of the forest, to the top of **Perley Combe**.

 ③

At the top of the combe, as you emerge from the trees, there is a wooden signpost indicating five different directions.

There is also a bench seat here, which you may well need by the time you get to it!

Follow the sign pointing to **Rodhuish** and continue along the track to reach the trig point at 1,248 feet above sea level.

Take your time to admire the views and watch out for buzzards and red deer.

Continue past the trig point, keeping in the same direction and heading downhill.

 ④

Where paths merge, turn right and almost immediately right again. This takes you onto a pleasant green path (a ride although signs declare no horses are allowed).

 ⑤

When the ride reaches the wide forestry road, turn left and immediately right to follow the forestry road gently downhill. Go straight across where a track crosses yours. You will see the far side of **Perley Combe** in front of you. This was the combe that you ascended at the start of the walk and it offers your return route.

 ⑥

Continue until the forestry road curves sharply around to the left at

The Royal Oak pub in Luxborough

a point where another forestry road doubles back to your right. Turn right onto that track and in a short distance, as the main track curves to the right, continue straight ahead onto a tractor track.

At point 6, you may prefer to extend your walk by following one of the many other paths through these woods. They are clearly marked on the OS map.

To return on the main route, follow the tractor track to a crossroads where you turn left, putting you back on your earlier path from where you retrace your steps to your car.

5 | Holford

The welcoming village pub at Holford

The Walk: 2 miles ⏰ 1¹/₄ hours
Map: OS Explorer 140 Quantock Hills & Bridgwater (GR 154411)

How to get there

Holford can be found on the A39 between Bridgwater and Minehead. The Plough Inn is in the centre of the village. Turn off the main road onto the lane that passes in front of the inn (not the narrow one behind it). Drive past the church, bearing left where a narrow road merges from your right. Bear right at the fork, signposted for Hodder's Combe, and turn left into the car park once the village green comes into view. **Parking:** The village green car park at Hodder's Combe. Patrons of the Plough Inn can use their car park.

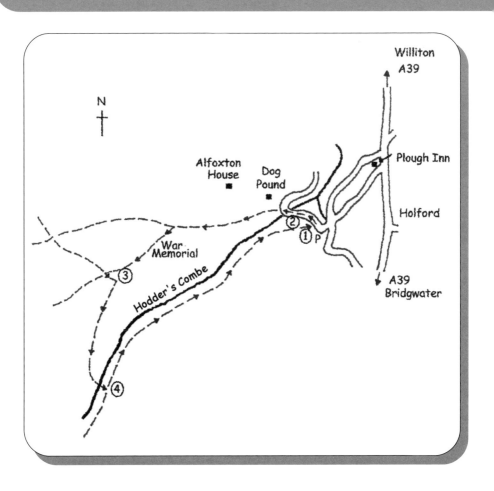

Introduction

Holford offers a delightful base for some of the best walking in Somerset. Its most picturesque corners lie tucked away from the main road, at the entrances to the many combes, with names like Butterfly Combe, Lady's Edge and Shepherd's Combe, which emanate from the 'Bowling Green' at the heart of the village.

The Plough Inn

The 16th-century Plough Inn is full of old world charm and offers an excellent selection of meals and real ales. There is an especially warm welcome for walkers and mountain bikers and nothing is too much trouble. The inn has non-smoking areas inside plus a section in which well behaved dogs are welcome. There is also seating outside. Some overnight accommodation is available. Telephone: 01278 741232.

THE WALK

From the car park entrance, turn left onto the metalled road with the village green (the **Bowling Green** as it is known) on your left-hand side. Where the road bears right, take the wide stone track leading straight ahead. This passes to the left of the old dog pound.

This is hunting country. The dog pound is where the strays were kept after a hunt. In years gone by, a pack of hounds were kept at Alfoxton House, the white house that you will see on your right as you ascend this path. The keeper of the hounds would hang meat from the trees to attract local stray dogs that unsettled his hounds. On one night, he went out to see what was disturbing the pack but forgot to put on his working clothes. The hounds mistook him for an intruder and killed him! To avoid a recurrence, the pound was built in which to keep any strays.

Continue along the uphill track, past the grounds of **Alfoxton Park**, and turn left onto a steep stony track which leads up to an isolated stand of pine trees.

Beneath these lies the village war memorial and the trees provide welcome shelter from which to look back at the views across the Bristol Channel and to the Mendip Hills.

Continue straight on, heading towards a rounded knoll at the hilltop before you, ignoring the grassy track leading off to your right.

Halfway between the war memorial and the knoll, you come to a crossroad of paths. Take the one that goes off to your left and drops down into **Hodder's Combe**. Follow this track all the way to the bottom of the combe.

Cross the stream and turn left to follow it downhill, keeping the water on your left-hand side, all the way back to the village green and car park.

THIS ANCIENT DOG POUND
WAS GIVEN TO
THE VILLAGE OF HOLFORD IN 1982
BY THE FAMILY OF THE LATE

JOHN LANCELOT BRERETON

DESCENDENTS OF THE St. ALBYNS
OWNERS OF ALFOXTON
SINCE THE 15th CENTURY
WHOSE CREST APPEARS ABOVE

The crest seen on the wall of the dog pound

6 | West Bagborough

The Rising Sun pub

The Walk: $3^{1}/_{2}$ miles ⏱ 2 hours
Map: OS Explorer 140 Quantock Hills & Bridgwater (GR 172334)

How to get there

From junction 25 of the M5 motorway, follow the A358 signs towards Minehead. Turn right at the West Bagborough turning and follow the road for $1^{1}/_{2}$ miles. The Rising Sun will be found on the left. From Williton or Minehead, take the A358 to Taunton, turning left into the village where signposted. **Parking:** Roadside parking can be found in the vicinity of the Rising Sun. Please park with consideration to local residents.

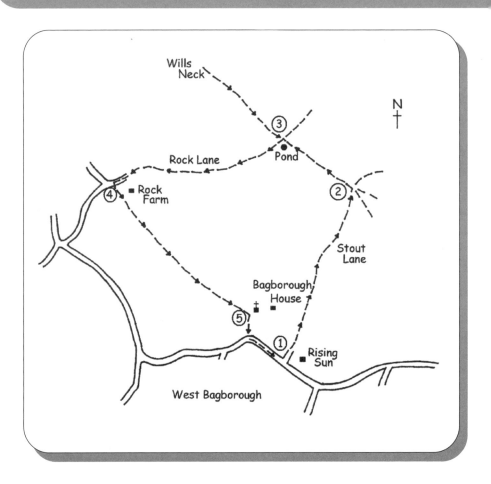

Introduction

This walk takes you around the south-western slopes of the Quantock Hills to Wills Neck, the highest point. These hills were the nation's first designated Area of Outstanding Natural Beauty. The walk passes along steep-sided wooded combes and open moorland. Watch out for red deer, wild ponies and buzzards. West Bagborough, referred to locally as just Bagborough, is a small hamlet dating back to Saxon days. It is believed that the name originates from Begas Barrow, Badger's Hill.

The Rising Sun

In the centre of the village is a 16th century inn renowned for the quality of its food, the Rising Sun. It's lucky to be there for in January 2002 it was destroyed in a devastating fire which required seventy-five firefighters from across the county. It has since been rebuilt and reopened and once again offers excellent meals and a good choice of local ales. Some overnight accommodation is available and well behaved dogs are welcome in the bar area. Telephone: 01823 432575.

THE WALK

Take the small lane, **Stout Lane**, which runs uphill alongside the **Rising Sun**, passing through a gate. Continue steadily uphill. In about $^3/_4$ mile, you reach the **Quantock ridge path** from where you can enjoy views across the Bristol Channel to South Wales.

On the way up this path, you will have clear views of Bagborough House and the village church to your left. Red deer are often seen grazing in these fields. The hills seen beyond the house are the Brendon Hills, the beginning of Exmoor.

Turn left onto the ridge path, keeping the wooded area on your left, and follow this for about 400 yards. Just before you reach the end of the wood, a path forks off to your right but you continue straight ahead following the yellow marker.

At the corner of the wood, notice the path going off to your left around the pond. This is your route on the way back. For now, continue straight ahead up over the moor to the trig point at **Wills Neck**.

Wills Neck, at 1,261 feet, is the highest point on the Quantocks. The views here are far reaching, taking in the wilds of Exmoor, South Wales and the Black Mountains and the Mendip Hills to the north-east. It is believed that Wills Neck takes its name from Wealas, which is what the locals once called the Welsh and it simply meant foreigners.

Retrace your steps to point 3 and there turn right, just before the pond, down the stony path marked with a circular disk, to descend the hill through the woods. You are now passing down **Rock Lane** along the western edge of **Bagborough Plantation**. Ignore the gated track which crosses your path and continue as the path descends more steeply down through a small wood, passing through a gate

The lychgate leading to St Pancras' church

partway down. Eventually you emerge onto a metalled road as you approach **Rock Farm**.

Walk past the farm, which will be on your left-hand side, to where there is a kissing gate on the left signposted as a footpath. Go through the gate, then straight ahead, with the farm again on your left-hand side. Bear slightly right towards an old tree and water trough alongside a gate in the hedge opposite. Go through the gate and across the top end of a narrow field to another metal gate and waymarked stile, and then continue ahead towards a small ridge.

Follow the right-hand field boundary to go through another metal gate. As you approach this gate, take note of the small barn three fields straight ahead and follow the obvious footpath across those fields to reach the barn.

As you approach the back of the barn, pass through a gate, turn left and immediately pass through another gate, which is waymarked. Go straight ahead by following the left-hand field boundary to reach a kissing gate. Go through that gate and continue straight ahead with the walled garden of **Bagborough House** on your left. Follow this path to reach the churchyard.

On reaching **St Pancras' church**, turn right to head down a tarmac path to the lychgate, which brings you out onto the metalled road. Turn left here and in about $1/4$ mile you are back at the **Rising Sun**.

Drive and Stroll

7 | Corfe

The charming traveller's caravan near Pitminster

The Walk: 4 miles 🕐 2 hours
Map: OS Explorer 128 Taunton & Blackdown Hills (GR 232197)

How to get there

The village of Corfe is $3\frac{1}{2}$ miles south of the centre of Taunton on the B3170. **Parking:** The church and war memorial are alongside each other on the main road through the village. Parking can be found, next to the war memorial, in Mill Lane.

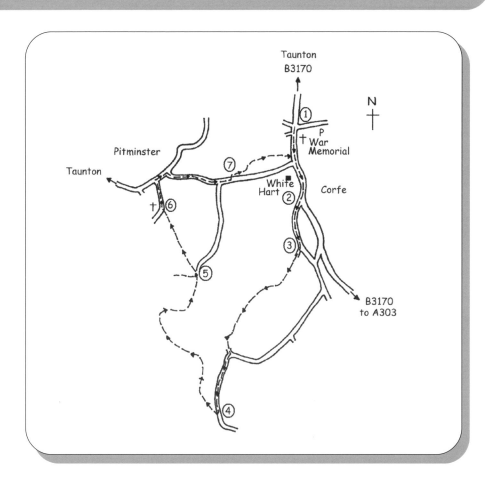

Introduction

The villages of Corfe and Pitminster lie in the Vale of Taunton Deane, on the edge of the Blackdown Hills. This pleasant walk takes in features from both of these, the meadows of the vale and the woodland of the hills. The high point comes at Adcombe Hill where splendid views of the Quantocks and Sedgemoor are revealed.

Corfe is one of those picturesque villages that so often serve as a dormitory for the nearby county town. Its church at the start of your walk is younger than its Norman appearance, being built in 1844. Nearby Pitminster, through which the walk passes, is the site of the discovery of a wooden chest containing a large quantity of French coins, intended to pay Monmouth's rebels in 1685.

Drive and Stroll

The White Hart Inn, Corfe

This traditional village pub and restaurant serves real ales and a range of meals. In fine weather seating is available outside on the terrace with views across to the Blackdown Hills. Telephone: 01823 421388.

THE WALK

From the war memorial, turn left onto the main road. Go past the **White Hart Inn**.

Turn right into **Adcombe Lane**. Follow this lane, ignoring the footpath to the right, until reaching **Adcombe Cottage**.

Immediately after Adcombe Cottage, turn right to head towards a gate. There is a house to your left and there is the feeling that you are entering someone's private grounds, but this is where the footpath goes, albeit not signposted. Pass through the gate and follow the track uphill as it hugs the left-hand edge of a wood. In about $1/2$ mile, ignore a wide track which goes off to your left and just keep going straight ahead until the track emerges onto a metalled road. Turn right onto the road in order to keep going uphill in the same direction.

In about 700 yards, just over the ridge of the hill, woodland comes up to meet the road from the right.

This is a good point to turn and look back at the view across the Somerset Levels and to the Quantock Hills.

At the start of the woodland is a gated entrance declaring it to belong to the **Woodland Trust** and bidding you welcome. Turn right here to pass through the gate and follow the track along the right-hand side of the wood. When the path forks shortly after entering the trees, ignore the track which drops off to the left, and just keep going straight ahead along more or less level ground, following the edge of the wood until the path drops down into the woodland. Continue to the end of the track, just after passing under some power cables, where it emerges by a cottage, which stands at the end of a metalled road.

Here you should find an interesting traveller's caravan, which dates back to about 1930. It belongs to the owner of the cottage who keeps it here as an ornamental feature. It is described as a Burton Vargas caravan.

The village pub at Corfe

  ⑤

The metalled road here goes to the right, across the front of the cottage, but you need to keep straight ahead into the signposted footpath track. In a short distance, the track ends at a gate. Cross the stile at the gate to enter a field. You will more or less follow the left-hand field boundary but bear slightly right to pass to the right-hand side of the barn, ignoring the two adjacent gates to the left of the barn. By following the left field boundary, you are heading to a double stile with a wooden bridge in between just to the left of the far corner of the field. Cross these and head straight towards the clearly visible church spire. This leads you to another stile, which takes you into the next field where you follow the path to emerge onto a metalled road in front of the church.

The church itself is well worth a visit. It contains memorials to the Colles family who once owned Taunton Priory.

  ⑥

Turn right at the road to reach a T-junction. Turn right here and in a short distance right again to follow the road signposted to **Corfe**.

Drive and Stroll

Continue along this road, ignoring the first footpath to the left, but picking up the footpath signposted to the left after **Fly Boat Farm**.

Leave the road by crossing the stile and turn immediately right to follow the field boundary, over another stile and into the next field. Follow the right-hand field boundary around this field until you reach a small pond.

Just after the pond, there is a large gap in the hedge. Pass through this and go straight ahead, crossing the large field, as you approach the now visible **Corfe village**. Partway across the field, following the obvious track, you pick up a hedged field boundary, which you keep on your left. This leads you back to the main road. You will see the **White Hart Inn** to your right as you approach the road. Turn left at the road to return to your car.

8 Hatch Beauchamp

The Palladian manor house of Hatch Court

The Walk: 3 miles ⏲ 1½ hours
Map: OS Explorer 128 Taunton & Blackdown Hills (GR 302205)

How to get there

Hatch Beauchamp is signposted eastwards off the A358 between Taunton and Ilminster, 4 miles from junction 25 of the M5 motorway. The Hatch Inn is in the centre of the village. **Parking:** The Hatch Inn offers parking for patrons and there are ample on-street parking opportunities as long as you avoid the junction.

Drive and Stroll

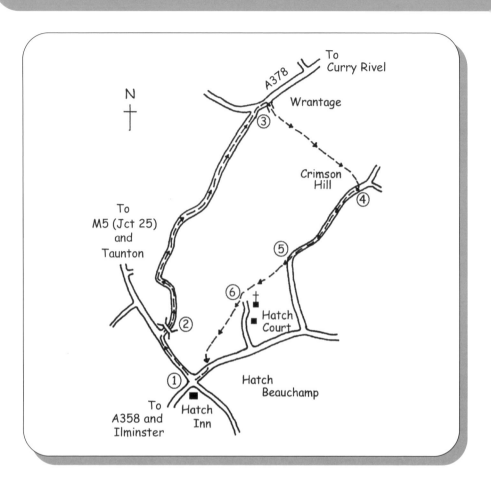

Introduction

Hatch Beauchamp (pronounced Beecham) is a small but well blessed community with a wonderful Palladian manor house, Hatch Court, surrounded by parkland within which nestles the village church. In the grounds of the church, alongside which you will walk, can be found the grave of Lieutenant Chard, hero of the 1879 battle of Rorke's Drift in the Anglo-Zulu War. The walk is very level with one moderate uphill slope. It passes along an old section of disused canal where a tunnel can be seen as it passes under the small hill you will climb before you stroll through the parkland of Hatch Court to complete the circuit.

The Hatch Inn

This friendly, family-owned village pub is a former 18th century coaching inn. It offers outside gardens, as well as a function room and a skittle alley. Children and dogs are welcome. There is a good selection of home cooked meals and en-suite accommodation is also available. Telephone: 01823 480245.

THE WALK

With your back to the **Hatch Inn**, head down the road signposted to Taunton.

In about 400 yards, turn right under a railway bridge and continue along this quiet road with the heavily wooded **Crimson Hill** to your right.

At the end of the lane, turn right onto the main road. Turn right again in a short distance before reaching the farm. Pass through a 7-bar metal gate onto a farm track. The track is quite rough in places having been filled in patches with builder's rubble. The path comes to a stile to the left and a gate to the right. Cross the stile immediately before you to continue along the same line of direction and towards the crest of the hill.

The family-owned village pub

The village church in Hatch Beauchamp

On your left you will be able to see where the now obsolete Chard Canal once ran and the entrance to the almost mile long Crimson Tunnel.

Continue along the path until crossing another stile, which brings you into an open field. Immediately before you, your onward path is visible just to the right of a small copse. At the top of the field are two Second World War bunkers and to the left of these is the exit from the

field over a non-dog-friendly stile (you will probably need to lift your dog over). Having crossed the stile, continue along the narrow track along the right-hand edge of a garden to emerge onto the road.

Turn right. In about ¹/₂ mile, as the road bears left, there is a large parking area to your right amidst the trees on the edge of **Line Wood**.

Here you will see a footpath sign pointing across a field with the tower of **Hatch Beauchamp church** visible on the far side. Head for the church and turn right on reaching a concrete roadway. When this splits, take the gravel path to the left, signposted as the footpath.

Continue forward between the buildings on your right and the church on the left. Passing through a small wicket gate, bear right, signposted in yellow as the footpath, keeping the hedge on your left and the field on your right.

Before doing this take time to visit the church. As you enter the churchyard, walk around the right-hand side and you will find the grave of Lt Chard just beneath the church wall. Chard was the brother of the rector and was living here when he died. He was one of two officers in charge of the famous defence of Rorke's Drift and was among the eleven men to receive the Victoria Cross on that day, the highest number ever awarded at one incident. Chard and his colleague Lt Bromhead were the central figures in the heroic action. There is also a stained glass window in the church to his memory.

As you continue along the path, away from the church, Hatch Court is clearly visible on your left. It is an elegant mansion house built with Bath stone. A herd of fallow deer graze the park.

At the end of the path, go straight across a road, which is the access road to **Hatch Court,** to continue along the signposted footpath, passing through a kissing gate. At the end of the path, turn right and before you will be seen the **Hatch Inn**.

9 Westonzoyland and the Battlefield

The Sedgemoor Inn, Westonzoyland

The Walk: 5½ miles 2½ hours
Map: OS Explorer 140 Quantock Hills & Bridgwater (GR 352348)

How to get there

Westonzoyland will be found on the A372 Bridgwater to Langport road, 3 miles east of Bridgwater. The spired church and the Sedgemoor Inn are almost next to each other on Main Road in the centre of the village. **Parking:** Kerbside parking can be found along Main Road in the church and village inn area.

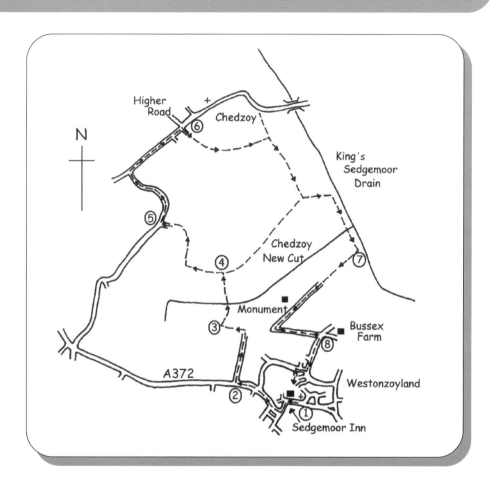

Introduction

This is a very level walk through dairy country, exploring the area in which the Duke of Monmouth fought the last battle on English soil in his unsuccessful attempt in 1685 to claim the throne from James II. It takes in the villages of Westonzoyland and Chedzoy, both of which boast fine churches in the Somerset Perpendicular style, each carrying the marks on the walls and doorways where the troops in the battle are reputed to have sharpened their swords.

The walk crosses a number of rhynes (pronounced reens), large man-made ditches, and for a stretch follows the river known as the King's Sedgemoor Drain.

Drive and Stroll

The Sedgemoor Inn

Dating back to the 16th century, this is a good country inn offering real ales and a wide choice of bar meals. The decorations inside include mementos of the Battle of Sedgemoor, including a framed copy of the Duke of Monmouth's admission to his illegitimacy, which he signed before his execution at the Tower of London. There is very limited space at the rear of the inn and it is best to use the roadside parking. Telephone: 01278 691382.

THE WALK

 ①

Walk from the church to the **Sedgemoor Inn** and continue along this main road as it bears left and then right at the village stores. Keep on this main road, heading towards **Bridgwater**, until you have passed the cemetery at the village edge, on the left-hand side.

Before leaving the church area, notice the old cemetery across the road. It contains the graves of thirteen RAF pilots who died between 1952 and 1954. They were being trained to fly the new jet-engined fighter planes, which suffered from an undetected fault. It was only after in excess of twenty deaths that the cause was discovered.

 ②

Turn right into **Penzoy Drove**. Go straight ahead along this drove until about 50 yards before it bears right. Turn left through a field gate and follow the left-hand field boundary straight ahead to reach a gap in the corner of the field.

 ③

Pass through the gap and turn immediately right to follow the right-hand field boundary until you reach the rhyne known as the **Chedzoy New Cut**. Cross the cut using the footbridge, which is slightly to your left as you approach the rhyne, and continue straight ahead following the right-hand field boundary.

 ④

On reaching a track (**Moor Drove**), turn left and follow it into the cluster of cottages at **Fowler's Plot**.

 ⑤

On reaching the village road, turn right and continue around to a T-junction where you turn right again to follow the road into the village of **Chedzoy**.

Before turning right at point 6 below, you may wish to pay a visit to Chedzoy church, which is a short distance ahead. This takes you past Higher Road and if you go a few yards down that road and turn right, the Manor Inn, which offers an alternative watering hole, can be found.

Memorials to those who lost their lives in battle

Drive and Stroll

⑥

Just before **Higher Road**, which is on your left, turn right into **Fry's Lane**, at the end of which is a gate. Cross the stile alongside the gate and go over the field to another gate to reach a track which crosses before you.

This is Moor Drove and is the route that Monmouth's rebel army took across the moor in 1685.

Turn right onto the drove and follow this until you reach a new drove where you turn left to head towards the **King's Sedgemoor Drain**, which you reach after passing through a field gate. Turn right just before the drain to follow the footpath, with the drain on your left-hand side. Continue straight ahead until, about 100 yards after crossing a bridge and sluice, you reach a field gate and stile. Do not go ahead over the stile.

⑦

Turn right to follow a long straight track to an angled T-junction.

Notice the memorial to those who fell at the Battle of Sedgemoor on your right-hand side, fighting 'for the right as they gave it'. The mushrooms around the memorial commemorate other battles: Trafalgar, Plessey, Quebec, Waterloo and the two world wars.

Turn left at the angled T-junction to follow the track to where it meets a metalled road at **Bussex Farm**.

⑧

Turn right here onto **Monmouth Road**, ignoring **Cheer Lane** on your left, and just after the **Bussex Stores**, turn left along a footpath which comes out at the back of the church onto the main road alongside the **Sedgemoor Inn**.

10 | Curry Rivel

The Burton Pynsent monument dominates the countryside

The Walk: 4 miles 🕐 2¹/₄ hours
Map: OS Explorer 128 Taunton & Blackdown Hills (GR 391252)

How to get there

Curry Rivel will be found 2 miles west of Langport on the A378. **Parking:** Entering from the Langport direction, the free public car park, which is conveniently beside the Olde Forge Inn, is signposted to your right behind the Sandpits Garden and Heating Centres.

Drive and Stroll

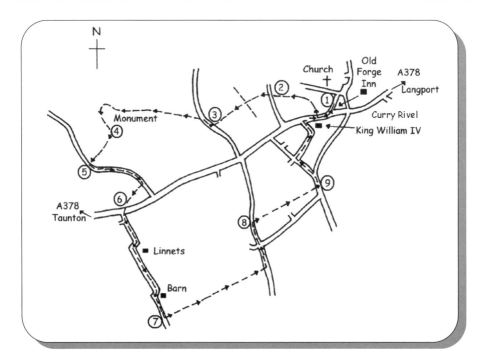

Introduction

Curry Rivel sits high on a ridge surrounded by the low-lying Somerset Levels. It is in the heart of willow-growing country where the withies are harvested annually to produce wicker furniture and baskets. The 15th century church, just uphill from the car park and alongside the picturesque village green, is well worth a visit. The first half of the route is dominated by the Burton Pynsent Monument and is rewarded by fine views to the north, whilst the return leg takes in the south side of this high ground, again with fine views.

The Olde Forge Inn

This characterful inn is housed within a Grade 2 listed building with a public bar, underground vaults and adjoining 14th century cellar bar. It is unusual in that it is a regular venue for art exhibitions. A choice of real ales is supported by an excellent menu catering for a wide variety of tastes and including fresh fish and vegetarian meals. They are closed on Sunday evenings and all day Monday but otherwise maintain normal licensing hours. Telephone: 01458 251554.

An alternative to the Olde Forge is the King William IV, which is passed just before the end of the walk. Telephone: 01458 251385.

THE WALK

On leaving the car park, turn left to drop down to the main road and turn right. Immediately after the post office, turn right into a narrow walled lane.

At the end of the lane, pass through a kissing gate and turn left onto the tarmac road, with the low stone building on your right. Cross the stile at the end of the path into a field.

Continue straight ahead keeping to the right-hand field boundary, a low stone wall. At the end of the field, cross the stone stile, road and kissing gate, which come in rapid succession. Continue straight ahead across the next field, following the left-hand field boundary. Go over the next stile (do not be tempted by the stile leading left) and follow the left-hand field boundary to cross another stile after which you follow the right-hand field boundary to emerge onto a road.

You should now be able to see the Burton Pynsent Monument to your right. Sir William Pynsent was a great admirer of William Pitt but was so scruffy he never got to meet him. But he left his fortune to Pitt and in return Pitt paid for the 140 foot high monument to be erected.

Turn right onto the road and in 100 yards, after **Dornford House** and immediately before the large metal gates of **Stoneleigh**, turn left onto a footpath signposted 'Swell $1^1/_2$ m, Moortown Lane'. Pass through the kissing gate into the field and follow the right-hand field boundary around to a stile, which leads to the monument.

Cross the stile and head for just right of the monument. Keep on this line as you pass the monument to drop down into a hollow on the far side. At the bottom of the hollow is a stile that leads into the woods. Cross this and drop downhill along the track until reaching the edge of the woodland where a stile tempts you to cross into a field. Ignore the stile and turn left before it to follow the path, which keeps you just inside the woodland.

After bearing around to the left, the path runs out at a field gate. Cross the stile alongside the gate into the field. The field dips before you and at the bottom, just to your right, is a small pond. Pass to the left of this pond and then head uphill, half right, to the clearly visible gate.

At the gate, turn left to go uphill along a tarred road. At the top of the hill you should see the traffic of the main road about 200 yards ahead. Halfway to the main road, cross a stile on your right into a field. Turn half left to go over the field, heading for some wooden frames near which is a stile leading out onto the main road.

Caution here please. The traffic is fast along this stretch and there is little room between the stile and the traffic.

Go straight across the main road into Moortown Lane. You will pass **Linnets** on your left, then a timber-built barn followed by an orchard.

Immediately after the orchard, turn left, signposted 'Holdens Way'. Follow the left-hand field boundary for two fields and continue straight ahead along a wide green track to reach a metalled road. Turn left and ignore the first turning to your right. After this the road bears around to the right.

As the road straightens up (just before where the power lines cross the road), turn right to go through a gap in the hedge, marked with a footpath post labelled 'Wiltown $\frac{1}{3}$ m'.

The village inn at Curry Rivel

The gap may be hard to spot, it is narrow and since the hedge arches over the opening, it is not immediately obvious.

Follow the right-hand field boundary to the next corner, at the back of a cottage garden, to find another, and difficult to spot, gap in the hedge. Follow the obvious path to reach a gate leading onto a road.

Turn left onto the road, left again into **Stoney Lane** and then right into **Bawlers Lane**. Follow this up to the main road where you turn right to return to the car park.

11 | Ilminster and Donyatt

Crossing the river as you enter Donyatt

The Walk: 3¹/₂ miles ⏲ 2 hours
Map: OS Explorer 128 Taunton & Blackdown Hills (GR 359145)

How to get there

From the Horton Cross roundabout on the A303, south-east of Taunton, take the B3168, signposted to Ilminster. Follow the road into the town centre, turn right into North Street and drive through into Ditton Street, following signs to the car park and public toilets. Turn right off Ditton Street between the garage and library, then right again into the pay and display car park, which backs onto the Red Cross centre. **Parking:** Public car park at the rear of the Red Cross centre. Some kerbside parking is available in the area. Parking is also available at the George Inn in Donyatt, the chosen inn for this walk, and is available for the use of patrons. Please consult the landlord if you intend to park and walk.

Drive and Stroll

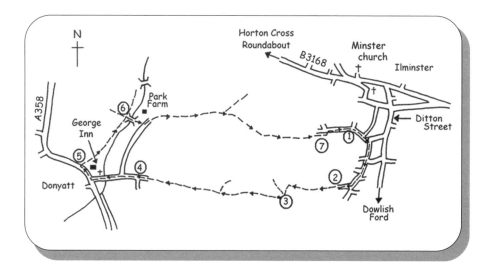

Introduction

The walk provides a fairly level route taking in pasture, woodland and riverside walking. The chosen inn is halfway around the circuit but it could be used as the start point if preferred. Ilminster offers a number of alternatives, including the Dolphin Inn, which is next to the minster church, St Mary's. The first part of the walk leads you to the site of a former canal, over the wooded Herne Hill, then across a disused railway into Donyatt. The return leg follows a river until once more crossing the old railway line to complete the route. These disused modes of transport reflect the one-time significance of Ilminster, which survives today as a quieter backwater bypassed by modern roads.

The George Inn, Donyatt

Dating back to the 16th century, this was almost certainly formerly a coaching inn. One end of the building was once a saddlery. Today the interior is light and spacious, with beamed ceilings from which hang assorted teapots and jugs. Real ales are served, alongside a wide selection of food. This popular inn offers a friendly welcome. Telephone: 01460 57518.

THE WALK

 ①

On leaving the car park, turn left onto **Canal Way** and then right into **Orchard Vale**. Proceed up the hill, with the playground on your right, into **Herne Rise**. After 34/36 Herne Rise, turn right into the cul-de-sac, at the top of which is a gap leading into a narrow field.

This narrow field is in fact the site of a disused canal. It was opened in 1841 and was part of a grand scheme to link the Bristol Channel from Bridgwater Docks to the Dorset coast and the English Channel. It failed to compete with the railways and closed in 1867. To your right at this point is the slope of The Incline. The canal traffic was moved up and down the hillside here, moving sideways rather than through a series of locks.

  ②

Cross this bottom end of the narrow field to reach a gate. Ignore the footpath to the left and proceed straight ahead, passing through the gate, into an enclosed lane with a large field sloping away to your right. Follow the path as it heads towards a wood. It eventually bears left with the trees on your right-hand side.

  ③

In 70 yards the path leads into the wood and immediately splits. Ignore the downhill path to the right and continue uphill. Follow the bold track along the left-hand edge of the wood, ignoring a stile on your left.

After passing a picnic table, your path starts to go downhill and in 20 yards another path crosses yours. Turn left here to go past a wooden bench and down to a kissing gate. Pass through the gate and follow the left-hand field boundary to the next gate and again follow the left-hand field boundary as it leads straight ahead towards the tower of **Donyatt church**. The path leads into a lane, which joins a metalled road.

  ④

Go straight ahead, over the disused railway bridge and river bridge, to reach the main road through the village. Turn right to find the **George Inn** on your right-hand side.

You will pass the 15th-century church on your right and along the main road can be seen six almshouses with mullioned windows, which date back to 1624.

  ⑤

Sixty yards after the **George**, turn right at the end of the houses to face a pair of field gates. Take the right-hand gate and bear diagonally right to cross the field to the opposite corner, down by the river. Go over the stile into the next field and follow the right-hand field boundary along the river bank through two fields until reaching a wooden bridge across the river.

Cross the bridge and go straight ahead through a gateway to follow the right-hand field boundary in the next field to emerge onto a gravelled track. Turn right and almost immediately left onto a tarred road, keeping **Park Farm** on your left-hand side.

Looking to your left, after the farm, you will notice a stretch of water, the partial remains of the former canal.

When the road splits, turn right, over the bridge and past **Coldharbour Farm**. Ignore the footpath signed to your left after the barns. Continue straight ahead to the end of the lane where you enter a field. Your way out of the field is diagonally across to your left in the far corner. Crops will almost

The George Inn, Donyatt

certainly dictate that you need to walk around the right-hand field boundary for two sides of the field to reach the kissing gate which leads out of the field into a short lane, at the end of which you pass through two more kissing gates in rapid succession.

After the second gate, continue straight ahead onto the tarmac path, with tennis courts alongside, and follow the footpath back to the car park. If you parked in **Donyatt**, then at the end of the playing fields, turn right as in point 1.

12 Ham Hill and Montacute

The Prince of Wales pub, Ham Hill

The Walk: 3 miles ⏱ 1³/₄ hours
Map: OS Explorer 129 Yeovil & Sherborne (GR 478168)

How to get there

From the A303 west of Yeovil, take the A356, signposted to Crewkerne. Take the first left, signposted to Stoke Sub Hamdon, and drive into the village centre. Turn right, signposted to Ham Hill, and then left, signposted to the Prince of Wales and car parks. **Parking:** Free parking is available around the Ham Hill Country Park. Parking close to the inn is for patrons only and is emphasised as 'when using the premises'. Alternative parking can be found on the other side of the road if none is found in the vicinity of the inn.

Drive and Stroll

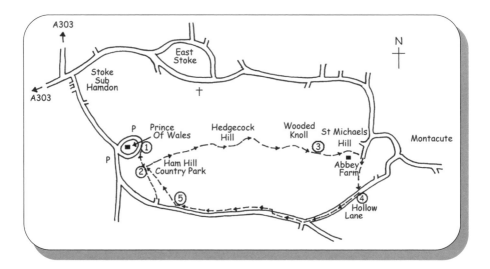

Introduction

The walk starts in the Ham Hill Country Park and travels through the woodlands of Hedgecock Hill towards the village of Montacute. The country park covers over 140 acres of woods and grassland surrounding the heavily quarried area you will notice as you set off. The quarrying dates back over 500 years and the undulation of the landscape bears witness to the activity with steep sided quarries and huge depressions.

Other activity on the site dates back to the Iron Age and evidence of Roman earthworks can still be seen on the ancient hill fort, which provides panoramic views across South Somerset. The park area is rich in wildlife with such rare plants as the bee orchid and autumn gentian.

The Prince of Wales

This 17th century inn sits in its isolated location in the heart of the park, close to the ranger's office. For centuries it served as a cider house for the quarry workers, and today it is an excellent country pub with bar and outdoor seating. Dogs are welcome. There is also a large restaurant area, the top part of which was formerly a chapel for the quarrymen.

The inn offers a good selection of real ales and a wide choice of food with fish, meat and vegetarian dishes on both the à la carte and speciality menus. Telephone: 01935 822848.

THE WALK

From the front of the inn, take the signposted path downhill towards **Montacute**. Ignore the footpath to the left signposted to **East Stoke** and go ahead with the quarry on your right-hand side. Continue straight ahead as a larger track merges from your right.

On reaching two stone carvings in a clearing (as illustrated), there are two paths to your left. Ignore the first, which is signposted 'Montacute 1¼ miles', and take the second to go past a sign declaring 'Danger steep quarry'. These two paths actually run in parallel, the left one on the lower ground and the right one (your path) on the higher ground.

Follow the path through an area of dips and banks, indicating former quarrying, into a wood.

The light-yellow stone carved from these quarries has been used all over Somerset but especially in the south of the county. Many of the villages in this area have chocolate-box cottages built with this local stone, which mellows to a wonderfully attractive fawn colour.

The path follows a stone wall for part of the way as you walk along the obvious track on the right-hand side of the wood, maintaining the same general direction for about ½ mile. A fenced path then merges from your right (enclosing a wood marked as private).

Go straight ahead following the fence line as a wooded knoll rises on your left. Continue on the track downhill and as the woodland on your right finishes, ignore the stile into the field to keep ahead, with the field on your right-hand side and the woodland on your left. In ¾ mile, the path forks. Turn right to enter the field over a stile.

The wooded **St Michael's Hill** will now be in front of you. Follow the line of telegraph poles to go straight ahead, passing just to the right of the wooded hill, along the right-hand field boundary. Shortly after your track rejoins the edge of the woodland, the path splits.

Continue left here if you wish to take a detour to the top of St. Michael's Hill where a tower can be ascended, providing magnificent views.

The left path follows the woodland edge and the right one leads into a gullied track, but just over the low bank on your right is a kissing gate. Go through this and follow the right-hand field boundary to pass along the left-hand side of the brick barn.

Drive and Stroll

Carvings sculpted from the fawn-coloured

Looking left here you can see the duck pond and the interesting buildings of Abbey Farm, which once served as the gatehouse to the nearby Montacute House.

Turn right at the end of the barn and pass through a gate to go straight ahead, slightly uphill to reach **Hollow Lane**.

You will soon be passing through a deeply cut ravine, which offers no passing places. But you soon emerge onto more open ground.

Turn right onto the metalled road heading back towards **Ham Hill**. Continue straight ahead as another metalled road merges from your left. You will soon notice that, on both sides of the road, the field gates carry 'Heritage Lottery Fund' signs. These gates give access to the fields allowing you to follow the road on the other side of the hedge line. Take any one of these gates on the right-hand side of the road and walk along the left-hand field boundary, which runs parallel with the road.

Eventually the field boundary leads you away from the road as it bears right, and ahead of you will be seen a stone plinth. Head for this to find three gates. Go through the right-hand gate, on the other side of which you will see the two standing stone carvings you passed on your outward journey. Walk just to the right of these to continue straight ahead (again ignoring the footpath to the right leading to **Montacute**) to retrace your steps back to the **Prince of Wales**.

13 | Brent Knoll

The village of Brent Knoll

The Walk: 3 miles ⏱ 1¹/₂ hours
Map: OS Explorer 153 Weston-super-Mare & Bleadon Hill (GR 330511)

How to get there

From junction 22 on the M5 go to the roundabout and turn right on the A38 towards Weston and Bristol. In ¹/₂ mile, turn left into village of Brent Knoll. The Red Cow is 1 mile on right. **Parking:** Kerbside parking is available in the vicinity of the Red Cow, which also has its own car park for the use of patrons.

Drive and Stroll

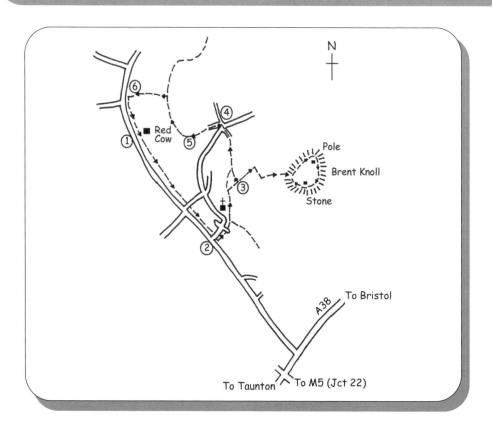

Introduction

Brent Knoll village was known as South Brent until around a hundred years ago when the railway arrived. The village is spread along the road that runs along the base of Brent Knoll, a hillock that rises to over 450 feet above the surrounding low-lying land. The Romans knew it as the Mount of Frogs, reflecting the marshland that once surrounded it as an island. On top of the knoll was an Iron Age fort. Brent is Saxon for 'beacon', and on the knoll a monument marks the beacon point.

The walk takes you from the low-lying Somerset levels to the height of Brent Knoll, a well-known Somerset landmark for any traveller along the M5. The start of the walk climbs rapidly over a clay-soil path which can be slippery after heavy rain and is hence best saved for drier weather. Because the knoll stands in stark contrast to its low-lying surrounds, it gives the illusion of being a long uphill climb – but it's easier than it looks, and the views on the knoll are ample reward.

The Red Cow

Dating back to 1670, the Red Cow, on Brent Street, offers a warm welcome and a friendly family atmosphere. A good selection of beers is complemented by a menu offering a wide range of meals. A children's room is available inside and a spacious beer garden outside. Internally, the inn is deceptively large and includes a no-smoking area. Telephone: 01278 760234.

THE WALK

With your back to the **Red Cow**, turn left to head south-east along **Brent Street**, with the knoll rising up to your left. Follow this road until you have passed the parish hall.

After the parish hall, turn left into **Church Lane**. Head straight up the hill before you. As the road bears left, take the kissing gate on your right onto the path signposted 'Public Footpath'.

This path can be quite slippery after prolonged wet weather but improves in a short distance.

The path forks just as you arrive at the back of the church. Walk to the left. After passing through another kissing gate, ignore the stile to your left and continue uphill to the next kissing gate.

Beyond the gate, the path splits. You will take the route to your left on

your return. To continue the walk, go straight ahead up the hill to reach the crest of the knoll.

From the summit of the knoll, there are extensive views to the Mendip Hills in the north, the meandering River Parrett in the south and the Bristol Channel and South Wales in the west beyond the coastal resort of Burnham-on-Sea. Take a walk around the summit. The presence of former massive defensive earthworks from the Iron Age are clearly visible. The knoll also served as a beacon hill and a monument commemorates three of Queen Victoria's jubilees, celebrated with beacon fires.

Once you have taken in the views, retrace your steps and turn right onto your return path just before the kissing gate. Follow the track to pass through a farm onto the metalled road.

Go straight across the road. To your left is a road indicated as 'Private road to Windy Ridge'. To the right of this road is a courtesy parking area, at the end of which is a gate. Pass through the parking space, and the

The pub on Brent Street

gate, and then follow the well worn path into the field. In about 50 yards, the field opens out. At this point head diagonally off to your right across the field towards the very top corner where you will cross a stile between the field gate and the back of a private garden.

  ⑤

After going over the stile, follow the left-hand field boundary to another

stile. Cross this and descend steeply down to the village, ignoring a stile halfway down on your left.

 ⑥

At the road, turn left to go along **Brent Street** and follow this road all the way back to the **Red Cow**.

14 | Wedmore

The River Axe from Bartlett's Bridge

The Walk: 4 miles ⏱ 2 hours
Map: OS Explorer 141 Cheddar Gorge & Mendip Hills West (GR 436479)

How to get there

Wedmore is situated where the B3139 between Highbridge and Wells crosses the B3151 between Glastonbury and Cheddar. The Swan Inn can be found where these roads meet. Directly opposite the Swan Inn is Church Street and a few yards along this you will find the George Hotel.
Parking: Kerbside parking is available in all the streets around the centre of the village.

Drive and Stroll

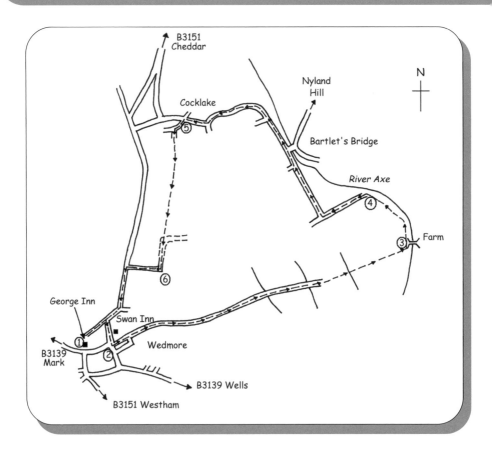

Introduction

The walk provides a level route across dairy meadowland and, for part of the way, alongside the River Axe. Whilst the route is low lying, the paths are fairly firm even after heavy rainfall.

Wedmore village, which grew up around a Saxon square, was once a shallow island standing proud from the surrounding marshes. As if raised on a second tier of higher ground, the church is situated on its own island. It was here that the Treaty of Wedmore was signed between the victorious King Alfred and the defeated Guthrum, the Dane, in AD 878. Nearby Mudgley Hill is believed to be the site of Alfred's royal palace.

The stone-built houses of the village are tightly packed with alleys and courtyards giving the whole place character and charm. Fashionable dress shops are a speciality here.

The George Hotel

A former coaching house, the 17th-century George Hotel offers a selection of real ales and home-cooked food, with an extensive choice of dishes, including vegetarian. Overnight accommodation is also available. Well behaved dogs are allowed in the bar area and in the attractive walled garden. Telephone: 01934 712124.

The Swan Inn provides an alternative to the George Hotel and has an easily accessed beer garden at the side. Telephone: 01934 712231.

THE WALK

From the **George Hotel**, walk downhill to the **Swan** and turn right.

Next to the George Hotel is the fine church, which is worth a visit. Also the courtyards and lanes where some excellent and unusual shops can be discovered.

Turn left into **The Lerburne**, opposite the **Borough Yard**. At the end of the metalled road, keep straight ahead on the obvious hard track. Follow the path past a farm. You will cross a rhyne (a wide ditch), and continue straight ahead through a metal gate, across another rhyne to reach a gate in front of you at the end of the lane.

To your left notice the distinctive shape of Nyland Hill, doing a modest impersonation of Brent Knoll featured in Walk 13.

Keep straight ahead here, passing through the gate, to follow the right-hand field boundary. Go over a ditch using a railway sleeper with a handrail. Continue straight ahead to cross the next ditch with a similar bridge.

Each of these footbridges has a metal plate halfway across indicating they are footpath routes.

Go straight ahead in the next field, following the left-hand field boundary, to reach and cross a double stile.

The rhynes and parallel ditches that criss-cross this area are essential to the drainage and irrigation of the low-lying fields, which without them would be flooded in winter and bone-dry in summer. Hence, the field sizes are never too large, since the moisture benefit needs to reach the centre in dry spells.

Turn left after the second stile to follow the bank of the **River Axe**, which you keep on your right-hand

The George Inn, Wedmore

side. At a point where power cables cross the water, the track bears left, then right and then left in rapid succession, finally to head away from the river. Go straight ahead, following the left-hand field boundary, towards a gate visible before you.

There are in fact two gates when you get there. Turn left here to go over the stile of the first gate and continue straight ahead until, in about 300 yards, you turn right onto a wide track to head towards the farm and, beyond the farm to reach **Bartlett's Bridge**. Keep straight ahead here, following the metalled road into **Cocklake village**.

Once in the village, the road meanders a while. Turn left

immediately before **Home Lane Farm**. Follow the track and turn left at **Crate Farm** on the signposted footpath. Go along a relatively short lane to reach a series of fields, which you cross by just walking straight ahead all the time through a series of waymarked gates and stiles, until emerging into a lane with a cemetery to your right.

Follow the lane as it bears right to take you up to the main road. Turn left.

Caution needs to be shown along this section of road. There is a pavement on the left-hand side for a section of this, but otherwise it is best to keep over to the right.

Walk back into the centre of **Wedmore village**.

15 | Priddy Mineries

Hurdles stacked ready for Priddy Fair

The walk: 4 miles ⏱ 2 hours
Map: OS Explorer 141 Cheddar Gorge & Mendip Hills West (GR 548513)

How to get there

On the B3135 between Cheddar Gorge and Chewton Mendip, turn south at the Miners Arms. **Parking:** Half a mile south of the Miners Arms junction, there is a Forestry Commission car park serving the Stock Hill plantation.

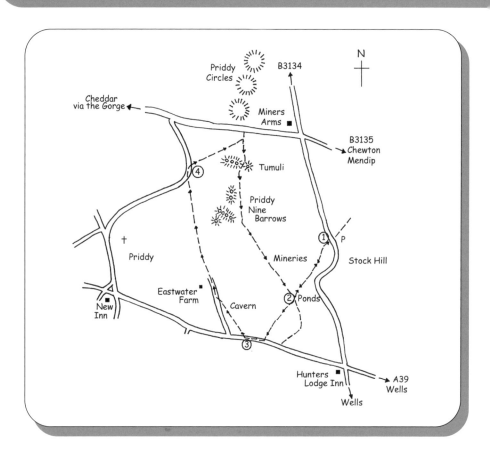

Introduction

This walk crosses the high moors of Mendip, passing through prehistoric sites where burial mounds abound and where once there was an active lead mining community. The mining has long gone and Priddy village today is noted for its annual sheep fair, which has been held here since 1348 when the plague drove it out of the nearby city of Wells. On the village green can be seen the thatched stack of 130 hurdles which once came into use for that annual event.

Caving and potholing are favourite sporting activities around here, so don't be surprised to see people in wetsuits appearing from nowhere since the walk goes through an area where many caverns and mine shafts can be found. Please note that these can be dangerous and under no circumstances should they be entered on your walk.

The Hunter's Lodge Inn, Priddy

This large and traditional rural inn, which is a short drive south of the Stock Hill car park, dates from the end of the 18th century. It is very popular with the caving fraternity who regularly meet here. The food – good basic fare – reflects the clientele who are in the main farmers, cavers and potholers, and walkers. Cottage pie, locally made faggots, pasta, chilli and vegetarian dishes are among the selection. The real ales in this excellent free house come straight from the barrels racked up behind the bar. There are two gardens with picnic tables and two bars, but such is the popularity of this inn that during the high season, meals are often eaten standing up. Telephone: 01749 672275.

Due to the popularity of the Hunter's Lodge, I include an alternative, the New Inn at Priddy, which sits on the village green – and it isn't new, it's quite ancient. Food is served at lunchtime and in the evenings. Children are welcome and there is an outdoor play area. Meals can be taken inside or outside in the garden area. Telephone: 01749 676465.

THE WALK

①

Leave the car park and cross to the road to follow the footpath opposite, which bears left to take you down through the **Priddy Mineries** which is a nature reserve.

 ②

On reaching a pond on your left, continue straight ahead to reach the metalled road. Turn right onto the road. In about 200 yards, after several houses, you come to a gate on your right.

 ③

Pass through the gate and head diagonally to the left in the direction of **Eastwater Farm**.

To your right you can see Eastwater Cavern in a low-lying part of the field.

Just after the farm, you emerge onto **Eastwater Drove**, which you follow northwards until reaching a metalled road (**Nine Barrows Lane**).

Turn right onto the metalled road and iturn right again through a stile to enter the field.

You will see a number of barrows on the high ground before you. These are what you are aiming for but they must be approached from the left-hand side as you view them.

Bear left to go uphill towards a gateway in the top left corner of the field.

Drive and Stroll

The Hunter's Lodge Inn, Priddy

You could go through the gate ahead of you at this stage to cross the road and examine 'Priddy Circles'. These are ancient henges dating back to around 2000 BC.

For the main walk, just before the gate, turn around to go to the right, almost doubling back on yourself, but now heading for the barrows on the ridge before you. Pass through this line of barrows and aim for a second set of barrows on the high ground, making for the corner of the field where the wall meets the fence. Cross the stile and walk beside the wall, keeping it on your right, following it down to the pond which you passed earlier at point 2.

The barrows are burial mounds and evidence of cremations has been found beneath them. Dips in the centre of the barrows indicate those that have been robbed over the centuries.

As you approach the pond, notice the uneven nature of the ground surface – showing where lead mines have collapsed and where slag from the mining activity has been stacked. Heaps of spoil from mining can be seen on your right.

Turn left at the pond to retrace your steps to the car park.

16 North Wootton

The 15th-century church at North Wootton

The Walk: 3 miles ⏲ 2 hours
Map: OS Explorer 141 Cheddar Gorge & Mendip Hills West. (GR 564418)

How to get there

From Pilton on the A361 between Glastonbury and Shepton Mallet, take the signposted road to the village of North Wootton. After passing the Crossways Inn and Motel, turn right into the High Street to find the church. **Parking:** Park alongside the church. There is also ample parking space at the Crossways for patrons of the inn and motel.

Drive and Stroll

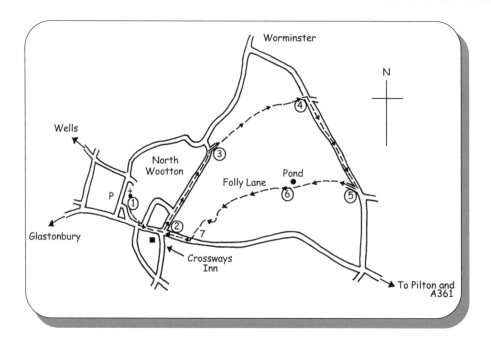

Introduction

This pleasant walk takes in the lower edge of the Mendip Hills with just one uphill stretch. It starts in the small farming village of North Wootton with its 15th-century church, village hall and green, all clustered together. Nearby flows the River Redlake, which the walk crosses, and the Whitelake, which meanders down to the Somerset Levels.

The Crossways Inn and Motel

This traditional Somerset inn has been considerably enhanced to become a hotel offering accommodation in 21 rooms. The original hostelry can be traced back to 1704 and, despite the modern atmosphere of the motel, the Crossways maintains the atmosphere of an old pub. There is a wide choice of meals from bar snacks to more substantial offerings and a daily specials board. Although dogs are not allowed inside, they can join you on the patio area with its far-reaching views. Telephone: 01749 899000.

THE WALK

Take the short road that runs alongside the church to cross the stream over a narrow arched bridge and turn right to follow the path down to the main village road. Turn left.

At the **Crossways Inn**, turn left into **North Town Lane**, signposted to **Worminster**.

In ¹/₂ mile turn right at **Trinity Cottage** to go past **Nut Tree Farm** and onto a rough track.

The start can be muddy after rain but soon improves. Notice the Mendip radio transmitter aerial over to your left.

Continue to the end of the track to where it reaches the metalled road at **Stoodly Bridge**.

The Crossways Inn and Motel

Turn right and ascend **Stoodly Hill**.

The distinctive Worminster Hill can be seen to your left.

At the top of the hill, turn right onto the signposted bridleway. Keep to the bridleway, ignoring footpath signs tempting you to the left. The path soon follows the left-hand edge of a fenced wood.

A small pond marks the end of the fenced stretch of woodland. In a few yards pass through a wooden gate.

Go through the next two fields following the hedge line, keeping to the same general direction, to reach the entrance into the third. At the third field, bear diagonally left to reach a stile, which leads into a lane. Follow the lane downhill to reach the village road.

Turn right to head back into **North Wootton**. You will go past the **Crossways Inn and Motel**. Turn right where a signpost points to 'Ford'. This takes you back to the church and your car.

17 Babcary

The Red Lion Inn at Babcary

The Walk: 2 miles ⏱ 1¼ hours
Map: OS Explorer 129 Yeovil & Sherborne (GR 565286)

How to get there

Babcary, near Somerton, is just east of the A37 between Shepton Mallet and Yeovil. Four miles north of the Podimore roundabout or 1 mile south of Lydford-on-Fosse, turn off the A37, signposted for Babcary. Follow the road to the Red Lion. **Parking:** There is a large car park belonging to the Red Lion. Patrons are welcome to use this but please consult the landlord before leaving your car while you walk. Alternative parking can be found along the roadside in the village centre.

Drive and Stroll

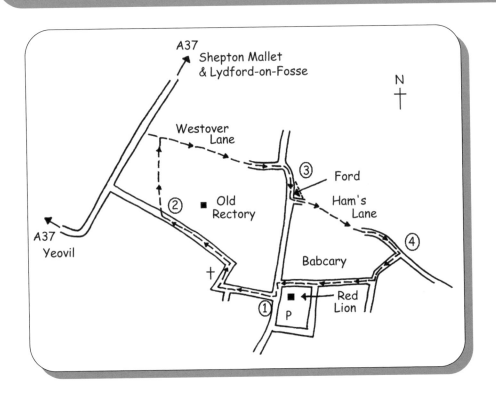

Introduction

Babcary is a small village near the Fosse Way, with fine houses built of blue lias stone and the River Cary passing through. The church, with its 15th century tower, once had Parson Woodforde as its vicar. He was famous for the diary that he kept during his term of service, a document that tells much about village life in the 1760s. The community was once self-sufficient. In 1861 it had a rector, baker, blacksmith, boot and shoe makers, cattle dealers, butcher, schoolmistress, shopkeepers, stonemasons, wheelwright and so on. This self sufficiency perhaps reflects its history as a village on an old drovers' route, Westover Lane along which the walk goes, being part of it.

The circuit is an easy one, short and very level. There are, however, one or two sticky patches that are better walked after a few days of dry weather.

The Red Lion Inn

This spacious and friendly village inn was once an 18th century farmhouse. The flagstoned and timbered bar is decorated with old prints of hunting scenes and a collection of books. At the rear is a newer restaurant area. An excellent menu is offered. Tables and chairs are set out in the lawned gardens and dogs are welcome there. Telephone: 01458 223230.

Babcary church where Parson Woodforde was once the vicar

THE WALK

Start the walk by heading back towards the A37, following the road signposted 'Charlton Mackrell 2'. After the church, the road bears left and crosses a stream. Continue until you have passed the **Old Rectory** (a large house set back from the road on your right) and the field next to it.

At the end of the field, turn right into a bridleway signposted 'Westover Lane 1/6 mile'.

This stretch has been heavily laid with builders' rubble to fill in the muddy stretches. It improves in a matter of yards.

Follow this track to its end at a T-junction. Turn right into **Westover Lane**. Continue along this green lane, ignoring a signposted track to your left. You will come to a ford.

Cross the ford using the stepping stones and turn left into **Ham's Lane**.

Beware, the stepping stones may be slippery and the water at times can be too deep. For a safer crossing, retrace your steps a matter of yards to a field gate that you passed earlier on your left. Enter this field, which belongs to the Somerset Wildlife Trust. Go half right across the field to an interpretation panel on the far side. Cross the footbridge over the ditch and turn left onto Ham's Lane.

Turn right on reaching the road. After ignoring a left turn, you soon reach **the Red Lion** where your walk started.

18 | Nettlebridge

The arched stone bridge near the start of the walk

The Walk: 2 miles ⏱ 1½ hours
Map: OS Explorer 142 Shepton Mallet & Mendip Hills East (GR 649484)

How to get there

Nettlebridge lies on the A367 between Radstock and Shepton Mallet. Approaching from the Radstock direction, shortly after a crossroads, take the left turning, signposted 'Nettlebridge', onto a narrow lane. Approaching from Shepton Mallet, turn right immediately after passing the Nettlebridge Inn on your right-hand side. Harridge Woods are on your left-hand side. **Parking:** Roadside parking is available at the gated entrance to the woods, opposite a cottage. Please park carefully so as not to block access to the woods or the narrow lane. The Nettlebridge Inn has a large car park for patrons, but you are asked to consult the landlord before leaving your car while you walk.

Drive and Stroll

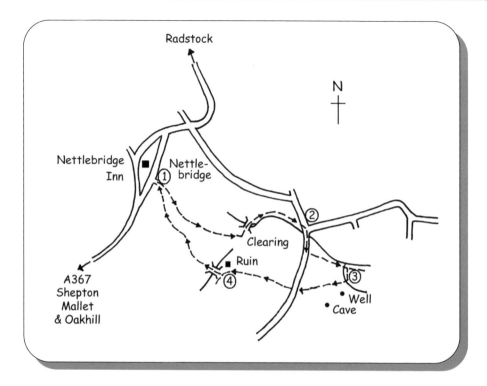

Introduction

This short but pleasant circuit begins and ends in Harridge Woods, with limited field walking at the turn around. Much of the woodland and the meadows through which you will pass are in the care of the Somerset Wildlife Trust, reflecting the importance of these deciduous woods. The little hamlet of Nettlebridge lies on the old Fosse Way, with the busy A367 now bypassing it with a loop, undoing the Romans' endeavours to keep the roads straight.

The Nettlebridge Inn

This free house, which offers en suite accommodation, was once an old coaching inn. It has a restaurant and bars plus the benefit of outside seating with views across the valley. Dogs are welcome in this area, which is tucked away around the back of the inn. There is a good choice of home-cooked food from the à la carte menu or the daily specials board. The inn is closed at lunchtime on Mondays but otherwise keeps conventional hours. Telephone: 01749 841360.

THE WALK

Enter the woods through the gated entrance and follow the obvious path for $1/2$ mile, ignoring any tracks to either side. On reaching a small circular clearing, turn left to head downhill and cross the stream over an arched stone bridge (as illustrated). Walk along the footpath with the stream on your right to reach a stile into a field. Follow the right-hand field boundary and cross the next stile onto a metalled road.

Turn right signposted 'Doulting'. In 80 yards, turn left into a sometimes hard-to-spot narrow and enclosed lane. It will be found between the transport yard and the field gate, almost adjacent to the yard. Follow the track until it crosses a stream, which cascades noisily down over a series of steps.

Turn right immediately after the stream and walk uphill beside the water to a gate, which will normally

The Nettlebridge Inn

be locked. Use the kissing gate to your left to get to the other side.

On your left now is St Dunstan's Well, which has been capped by Bristol Waterworks. The water gushes up here, thanks to a fault line in the rocks. The nearby St Dunstan's cave is 60 feet long and rises by 10 feet along its length. Medieval pottery has been discovered here suggesting that it could have been a Black Death burial pit.

Turn right at the well to follow the right-hand field boundary to a metalled road. Cross the road and take the gate immediately opposite into the Wildlife Trust **Limekiln Fields Nature Reserve**. The path bears left,

following the woodland edge to your left, down to a kissing gate, through which you pass. Keep straight ahead along the left-hand field boundary until reaching the next gate to enter the woods.

Beyond the ruined building, just inside the woods, the track splits. Take the right-hand path, signposted to Nettlebridge. Cross the wooden footbridge and go straight ahead up the stepped pathway to reach a T-junction with a forest track. Turn left to follow a stony trail down to the next T-junction where you turn left to reach the road and the parking spot.

19 | Nunney

The George Hotel, located near the castle

The Walk: 3 miles ⏱ 1½ hours
Map: OS Explorer 142 Shepton Mallet & Mendip Hills East (GR 737457)

How to get there

Nunney is 4 miles south-west of Frome. On the A361 road from Shepton Mallet to Frome, at the roundabout junction with the A359 road to Bruton, take the signposted turning into Nunney. The castle is unmistakable in the centre of the village and close by is the George Hotel. **Parking:** There is free parking limited to two hours in the market place, as you approach the George Hotel, but this may leave slower walkers tight on time. Alternatively, as you enter Nunney, turn left over the arched bridge into Castle Hill. The first turning right leads to the castle, which is clearly visible before you, and offers kerbside parking. Roadside parking can also be found in a layby a short way up Castle Hill at the end of a footpath.

Drive and Stroll

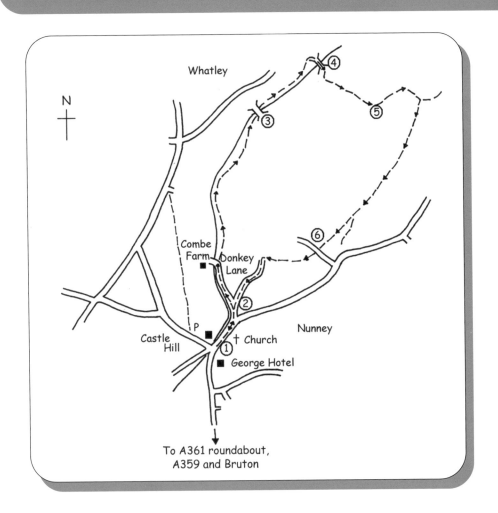

Introduction

Nunney is a quiet village at the edge of the Mendip Hills with an attractive collection of stone-built houses. The dominant feature, however, is the ruined and moated castle, much of which remains intact. It was built in 1373 by Sir John de la Mare. During the English Civil War, it was a Royalist stronghold and was subsequently destroyed by the Parliamentarian forces.

This is a fairly level and very pleasant walk, which follows Nunney Brook through woodland until the return path is taken across farmland and back to the village.

The George Hotel

Conveniently placed close to the castle, the George was once a coaching inn. Despite the ghost that is reputed to haunt its grounds (the gardens are believed to have been once used for executions), it still offers a friendly welcome – except for dogs, which are not permitted. However, across the quiet road from the inn are riverside tables for patrons of the inn and dog walkers could use these.

The food is excellent and the inn is well known locally for its steaks, Scottish beef and fresh fish, which is delivered daily from Cornwall. There is a good selection of real ales. Telephone: 01373 836458.

THE WALK

Start the walk by having a stroll around the castle where the admission is free. Across the road is the church, which can be reached by leaving the castle across a footbridge over **Nunney Brook**. Turn left, as you face the church, to go 80 yards up the road.

Take the first turning left into **Donkey Lane**. Keep straight ahead, ignoring a track off to your right which will be your return route. Go through a gateway onto the drive to **Combe Farm** where a footpath sign points straight ahead. When the lane bears left to the farm, keep straight ahead through a kissing gate to follow the bottom of the combe with **Nunney Brook** on your left.

In ³/₄ mile, a track crosses your path. Turn left here, following the footpath sign, to cross the stone bridge. Once over the bridge, turn right and continue in your previous direction but now with the stream on your right.

Notice the cross-country fences along the way, showing where three-day event horses are trained.

In just under ¹/₄ mile, the path climbs away from the stream to join a track higher up. Turn right onto the track to cross an arched bridge back over **Nunney Brook**. The track leads through a gate with the footpath signposted straight ahead. In 40 yards, turn left through a field gate with a yellow painted arrow. Follow the right-hand field boundary, heading for the field straight ahead. Enter the next field through the gate with a blue arrow.

Nunney Castle

Follow the left-hand field boundary to a stile into the field on your left.

Cross the waymarked stile and turn half right to head towards where the top of a tree is just visible over the brow of the rise in front of you. On reaching the opposite hedgerow, turn left and follow the right-hand field boundary to reach a stile in the corner of the field. Turn right here to enter the next field and follow its left-hand field boundary to the next corner and enter the next field at a waymarked stile.

Turn half right, as shown by the arrow on the stile, to reach the far hedgerow where a stile is just visible. Cross the double stile into the next field and follow the left-hand field boundary, past a field gate, on to the corner of the field where there are adjoining entrances into two other fields. Take the stile into the field on your left, turn right and follow the right-hand field boundary to the next corner.

Cross two stiles, and a farm road, to continue straight ahead into the field opposite, again following the right-hand field boundary as waymarked. Immediately after a large gap in the hedgerow, cross a stile in front of you to enter a narrow bowered lane. Follow this all the way, through two kissing gates, down to **Donkey Lane** where you turn left to retrace your steps to your car, passing the **George Hotel** on your left-hand side.

20 | Cleeve and Goblin Combe

The Lord Nelson pub at Cleeve

The Walk: 5 miles   🕐 2¹/₂ hours
Map: OS Explorer 154 Bristol West & Portishead (GR 458654)

How to get there

Cleeve is found on the A370 main road between Weston-super-Mare and Bristol, 1¹/₂ miles north of Congresbury. The Lord Nelson is a large building on the main road that you cannot miss. Take the side road adjacent to the inn, Cleeve Hill Road. **Parking:** About 400 yards from the main road there is an easily found free car park on the left-hand side immediately after a turning to the left.

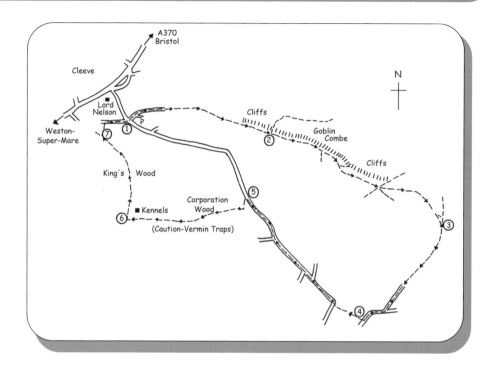

Introduction

Although this is one of the longer circuits, it is easy walking with all inclines being relatively gentle. The outward journey passes through Goblin Combe, which is as magical as its name suggests. Among the predominant ash there are many native fir trees with wonderfully gnarled trunks and root formations, brought about by their struggle to penetrate the rocky soil. In the upper reaches, the invasive sycamore is making its presence felt. Limestone cliffs and crags line the left-hand side and large boulders, broken off by the action of ice, lay strewn alongside the pathways. A $1/2$ mile stretch of this combe can be muddy but passable after wet weather, so the walk is a good one to do during a hot, dry spell since the greater part of it is through shade-providing woodland.

At the turn – around point, the route passes through open countryside before entering woodland to complete the trip. For those considering a picnic, there are a number of seat-sized tree stumps just inside Corporation Woods on the return leg.

Drive and Stroll

The Lord Nelson

This large freehouse on the main A370 through Cleeve is spacious inside and offers a garden area to the rear with a children's play area. Seating is also available outside at the front. It is definitely a family-friendly inn. The menu includes grills, fish, scampi, with occasional promotional offers. Telephone: 01934 832170.

THE WALK

Leave the car park and turn right onto the road and right again into **Plunder Street**. Pass along the front of the **Goblin Combe Centre** taking a waymarked footpath between two pillars to follow a walled lane through a gate with a notice 'Walnut Tree Farm. Footpath to Wrington only'. Continue straight ahead as this becomes a dirt and stone track.

Notice the high cliffs along the left-hand side of the combe. These are limestone rocks, which allow water through them. The winter frosts then expand the water as it freezes, causing large chunks of rock to break away. These are strewn along the path you will be following.

Ignore all paths leading to left and right and just continue straight ahead to pass through a gap in a stone wall, on the other side of which is a map board showing walks through the woodland.

Your route lies straight ahead but there is a diversion you could take

here if your energy levels are high. A stepped path leads steeply uphill, at the top of which you can turn right to go along the upper edge of the cliff and then take a path back down to rejoin your route. These tracks are indicated on the board. For a more leisurely stroll, continue as below.

Continue straight ahead, ignoring first the track to the right and then the one to the left at an **Avon Wildlife Trust** board. Continue ahead to a clearing at a junction of paths with a 'Goblin Combe Woodland' interpretation board. The main track here goes to your left but you need to go straight ahead, taking the left of the two lesser tracks before you (ignoring the one on the right which leads uphill). Following the left of these two tracks takes you along a green ride with higher ground on both sides.

You should by now be hearing the regular rumble of aircraft taking off and landing at the nearby Bristol airport. Don't be surprised to see them flying very low over the trees as you reach the higher ground.

Follow the track to where it splits and take the bolder track to the left to immediately pass a wooden pole barrier onto a T-junction with a farm trail.

Turn right and follow the woodland edge and then beyond the woodland to reach another T-junction. Turn right and then follow the lane as it bears left.

Eighty yards after the bend, turn right to go through a kissing gate and follow the footpath across the field, going straight ahead as indicated.

Although footpaths across cropland are often obscure, this one has always been well defined on my visits.

Turn right on reaching the metalled road and follow this for just over $1/2$ mile.

After passing through a stretch where there is woodland on both sides of the road, turn left at **Woodside Cottage** to take the signposted footpath into **Corporation Woods**. Follow the obvious track into the woods as the path bears right at some chicken runs.

Caution – please take note of the warnings to keep dogs on leads through this woodland as a number of vermin traps have been set. This does not apply once you reach King's Wood.

Follow the track past a bungalow and then past the dog kennels.

After the kennels and the white-painted house, turn right before the barn onto a waymarked track and go straight ahead by **Woolmer's Cottage** to enter **King's Wood**. Continue straight ahead on the obvious track, crossing a wooden footbridge. In 20 yards, turn left where the path splits, following the waymarked footpath onto a track which leads you downhill.

In spring this area is thick with bluebells and wild garlic, the subtle smell of which you may well pick up long before entering the wood.

Leave the wood by crossing a stile into a field. Bear right to follow the right-hand field boundary down to a stile, which leads into the top-end of a lane. Turn right onto the lane to reach the car park.